# NIKKY'S KITCHEN COOK BOOK

A COLLECTION OF SIMPLE NIGERIAN DISHES RECIPES

## BHILQEES ADENIKE ALAUSA

Print information available on the last page

Rev. date: 03/20/2018

To order additional copies of this book, contact:
Xlibris
1-888-795-4274
www.Xlibris.com
Orders@Xlibris.com

The book comprises of simple Nigerian recipes that can be easily interpreted by everyone. The book guides readers on how easy it is to make some Nigerian delicacies.

The book uses US cup measurements, and the spoon measurements are leveled. The time for cooking is only used for a guide. The cooking time may be slightly different due to the type of cooking stove that was used. The color and taste will come out based on individuals' preference.

The recipes in this book can also be used by non-Nigerians.

# Table Contents

## Rice Dishes

## Beans Dishes

## Spaghetti Dishes

## Yam Dishes

## Soup

# Rice Dishes

# Jollof Rice

This is a special meal in every Yoruba homes and parties. Yoruba is one of the ethnic groups in Nigeria. It is said that a Yoruba party is incomplete without Jollof Rice. The food is made with Rice, bell peppers, tomatoes, onions and seasoning. It is slow cooked. Jollof rice can be eaten with fried plantain, chicken (grilled or fried), fish (fried or grilled).

## Ingredients

- 2 Red bell peppers
- 6 cups of un-cooked Rice
- 3-4 cups of Warm Water
- 2 8oz of Tomato sauces or 3-4 fresh tomatoes
- 1 6ozof tomato paste
- 1 Habanero pepper

- 1 bulbs of Onion
- 1 whole tomato
- 4 cubes of Knorr
- 1 cup of Oil
- 1 tea spoon of Curry
- 1 tea spoon of Thyme
- 2 table spoons of Butter

Time to cook – 1hr: 37 minutes

## How to Cook

1. Put the Red peppers, Habanero pepper, ½ onions, 4 cubes of knorr and the tomatoes or tomato sauces in the blender and blend till it is finely smooth. Then set it aside.

2. Heat the oil in a pot on a medium heat

3. Add the curry and thyme and let it fry for 20 seconds

4. Pour in the blended peppers with the tomatoes paste, stir until it is well mixed then cover to cook for 10 minutes.

5. Add the butter to give it a nice taste and flavor. Stir the mixtures together till the butter is no longer visible.

6. Cover and let it cook/fry for 20 minutes.

7. While the mixture is cooking, slice the whole tomato and the remaining ½ onions, then add both into the mixture.

8. Stir it intermittently to avoid it sticking at the bottom of the pot.

9. After 20 minutes, add the warm water, stir to the bottom and cover to cook for 2-3 minutes.

10. Add the washed un-cooked rice; make sure to stir the mixture again before adding the rice.

11. Reduce the heat and let it cook for minutes

12. Check to see if it is soft enough to eat and the water is dried, if not add little and do not increase the heat.

13. If you are not satisfied with the taste, add additional butter as this will enhance the taste as well as soften it.

14. Use wooden spoon to mix the rice and the pepper mixture together. Once you are satisfied with the taste and softness, then it is ready to eat.

# Hint

- Avoid adding plenty of water as this will make it soggy.
- Jollof rice needs to be cooked at medium eat to avoid it burning.

# Fried Rice

Fried rice is a healthy meal as it contains lot of vegetables (Corn, peas, carrots, etc.). It is usually stir fried and best cooked in a Wok. It can be eaten with plantains, chicken, grilled fish and meat.

## Ingredient

- 3 cups of rice
- 3-4 cups of mixed vegetables (carrot, green beans, peas, corn and snap beans)
- ½ cup of oil
- 2 stock cubes
- 2 tablespoons of butter

- 2 tablespoons of Curry
- 1 table spoon of Thyme
- 1 tablespoon of parsley flakes (optional)
- 10 Shrimps
- 1/2 bulb of onions to be sliced

Time to cook: 40-45 minutes

## How to cook

The First step is to parboil the rice (That can be done in a rice cooker).

1. Pour the washed rice in a rice cooker and add 2 cups of water with the seasoning (1 cube stock) along with 2 tablespoons of oil. The oil will prevent the rice from sticking together.

2. Allow to cook for 15 minutes or till almost soft.

3. If the rice is getting soft and there is still water in it, open so the water will dry out without over softening the Rice.

4. Once the water is dried and the rice is soft but not too soft, pour the rice into a bowl and put in the fridge to lock in the seasoning.

The next is the mixed vegetables. Using a Wok makes the stir frying easy due to its oval shape

1. Pour the oil in the Wok or Pot and heat for 3 minutes; add the onions, curry, thyme, parsley and sauté for 1 minute.

2. Then add the mixed vegetables with the remaining 1 stock cube, stir so the vegetables are well mixed with the curry and thyme. You can add little water to cook the mixed vegetables.

3. Stir intermittently to avoid the vegetables from sticking to the bottom of the pot or wok.

4. Cook for 15-20 minutes or till it's soft then add the shrimps to soften a little bit.

5. Now is time to pour in the cold rice, add the butter and stir fry till the rice and vegetables are well mixed on a reduced heat.

6. Taste to see if it is soft enough and well-seasoned. If not butter can be added or little salt or stock cube.

7. Once you are satisfied with the taste, then it is ready to eat.

# Hint

If it is not soft enough, add little water but do not cover it.

Wooden spoon or spatula is advised to be used.

# Beans Dishes

# Beans cake

This is made with beans, red bell pepper, habanero and onions. The native name is akara. It is one of Nigeria meals. It can be served during breakfast, lunch or dinner. It can be taken with oatmeal, custard or soaked garri.

## Ingredient

- 1-2 cups of beans
- Water
- 1 egg
- A pinch of curry (optional)
- 1 knorr stock or salt
- 1-1 ½ Red bell pepper

- 1-2 Habanero pepper
- 1 bulb of small onion (for blending)
- ½ small bulb onions (chopped) – (optional)
- 4-5 cups of oil (for deep frying)
- 5-6 shrimps (cleaned and chopped)

## How to cook

1. Soak the beans till the shell can be easily peeled off.

2. Remove all the beans shells and clean thoroughly

3. Blend the beans with the Red bell peppers, habanero peppers, onions, and ½ cup of water till the mixture is well smooth like a paste. The paste should be slightly thick.

4. Pour into a deep bowl; add the seasoning, the chopped onions, curry, crayfish and egg. Then mix them together.

5. Pour the oil in the pan and heat for 1-2 minutes, toss in a slice of onions to give it flavor.

6. Reduce the heat a little bit to avoid the beans cake from frying without getting well cooked.

7. Scoop the beans mixture into the heated oil with table spoon and set the heat to medium.

8. Let it fry till you get the dark golden color but not burnt.

9. Bring the beans cake out and eat with bread, pap, oatmeal, garri or your preference.

Hint: The added eggs makes the beans paste to easily mold together, gives it that definite shape and a smooth look.

# Beans and Stew (ata agoin)

Beans - This is a meal that is not only eaten by Nigerians but other African countries eat this food. It is cooked in different form; it can either be cooked plainly or be cooked with stew.

## Ingredient

- 2-3 cups of beans
- 4 cups of water (or as required)
- 2 knorr stock cubes
- 4 tablespoons of oil (optional)
- Pressure cooker (optional)
- Stew (ata agoin) - Ingredient
- I small tin of tomato paste

- ½ cup of oil (it can be adjusted as needed)
- 2 tablespoons of blended crayfish
- ½ cupe knorr stock cube or pinch of salt (the salt can be adjusted)
- 1 small stock of chopped onions
- ½ - 1 tablespoon Dry pepper (this can be adjusted)

## How to cook

1. Beans - Add water into the pressure cooker or regular pot; add the washed beans, and the other ingredients along with some sliced onions (this hasten up the softening of the beans).

2. Allow the beans to cook for 20 – 30 minutes or till it is soft. If there is still water in the cooked beans and it is soft, drain the water. Once all the water is drained, pour the beans into a dry pot add 4 table spoons of oil (optional) and heat up for 2-3 minutes. The beans is ready ☺

## Stew (ata agoin) How to cook

1. Get a clean pan, add the oil and heat for 1 minute, then add the onions. The onions should simmer for few seconds.

2. The next thing will be to add the tomato paste along with the dry pepper. Stir till the two are properly mixed, let it fry for 2 minutes.

3. Then add the blended crayfish. Stir all the mixture till it is well blended. Add the stock or salt. Let it fry and continue stirring as well to avoid the stew getting burnt.

4. Let the stew fry till the taste of the tomato paste is gone. It can be on the heat for 30 – 45 minutes. The longer it fries, the better the taste☺.

5. Enjoy the beans and stew with fried plantains, bread or eat it alone.

# Spaghetti Dishes

# Mixed Vegetables Spaghetti

This is a combination of spaghetti and mixed vegetables.

## Ingredient

- 1 box of Spaghetti (1.0 pound)
- Pasta sauce – 4-5 tablespoons
- ½ - 1 stock cube (knorr)
- 1 pack of mixed vegetables (16 ounces)
- 3/4 cup of oil
- 8-10 cups of water
- 1 teaspoon of salt
- ½ teaspoon of Curry
- ½ teaspoon of Thyme
- ½ teaspoon of Parsley flakes
- Chopped onions (optional)
- Sieve
- Pot

Cooking time 10-15minutes

## How to cook

1. Fill a large pot with water, add salt, put it on the stove and turn on the flame high till the water start boiling.

2. The next will be to pour in the mixed vegetable, reduce the flame to medium and allow the mixed vegetables to cook for 1 minute, and then add the spaghetti along with little oil. The oil is added to avoid the spaghetti from sticking.

3. Now let it cook till it's a bit soft but not too soft, usually 6 – 10 minutes. Please do not cover the pot with the lid so as to avoid the boiling water spilling into the stove.

4. Once both the spaghetti and vegetables are soft, pour into a sieve and allow the water to drain off.

5. While the water is draining, clean the pot to dry off the water then put the pot back on the stove on a medium heat.

6. Add the oil (the oil quantity can be adjusted), curry, thyme, chopped onions, parsley flakes, stock cube and the pasta sauce. Stir till they are well mixed and let it fry for 1-2 minutes.

7. The spaghetti should be well drained now, add the spaghetti into the sauce and mix thoroughly but gently to avoid shredding the spaghetti. Let it fry-cook for 1-2 minutes. Adjust the seasonings as needed.

8. Serve with chicken, beef, plantain or your preference ☺

# Jollof Spaghetti

This is a combination of spaghetti and tomato sauce.

## Ingredient

- 1 box of Spaghetti (1.0 pound)
- Pasta sauce – 10 tablespoons
- ½ - 1 teaspoon of dry pepper
- ½ - 1 stock cube (knorr)
- 3/4 cup of oil
- 8-10 cups of water
- 1 teaspoon of salt
- 8-10 tablespoons of corned beef

- 2-3 beef suasages to be sliced
- Curry
- Thyme
- Parsley flakes
- Chopped onions (optional)
- Sieve
- Pot

## How to cook

1. Fill a large pot with water, add salt, put it on the stove and turn on the flame high till the water start boiling.

2. Reduce the heat to medium and then add the spaghetti along with little oil. The oil is added to avoid the spaghetti from sticking. Now let it cook till it's a bit soft but not too soft, usually 6 – 10 minutes. Please do not cover the pot with the lid so as to avoid the boiling water spilling into the stove.

3. Once the spaghetti is slightly soft, pour into a sieve and allow the water to drain off. While the water is draining, clean the pot to dry off the water then put the pot back on the stove on a medium heat.

4. Mix the pasta sauce and dry pepper, and then add it into the heated oil along with curry, thyme, chopped onions, parsley flakes, stock cube, corned beef and sausage beef. Stir all gently till they are well mixed and let it fry for 5-10 minutes. Stir intermittently to avoid the sauce sticking to the bottom of the pot.

5. The spaghetti should be well drained now, pour the spaghetti into the sauce and stir with care to avoid shredding the spaghetti.

6. Let it fry-cook for 1-2 minutes. Adjust the seasonings as needed.

7. Serve with chicken, beef, plantain or your preference ☺

# Porridge (Asaro)

This is a meal prepared with yam. It is made in different ways, some add vegetables to it and some do not. In this book, we will not be adding vegetables.

## Ingredients

- 1 tuber of medium size yam
- 2 medium size bell peppers
- 1 habanero (it can be adjusted)
- 1 bulb of onion
- ½ cup of oil
- 1-2 cubes of know
- ½ teaspoon of salt (optional)
- 6-8 tablespoon of corned beef (optional)
- 1 tablespoon of sugar (optional)
- ½ teaspoon of curry (optional)
- Water

## How to cook

1. Peel the skin off the yam and cut into cubes (this is done, so it will be easily mashed and the sauce can get inside easily)

2. Pour the cut yams into a clean pot, add the know cubes, salt, sugar and fill the pot with water. Make sure that the water does not go above the yams.

3. Taste to be sure the seasoning is enough, more can be added if need be.

4. Cover and let it cook till in a medium heat till it is a bit soft but not soft enough to be eaten.

5. While your yam is cooking, blend the peppers with little amount of water (Bell peppers, habanero and ½ bulb of onion). Blend till it is well smooth

6. If the yam is slightly soft, check to be sure the water is not too much. If it is, take some out and retain it as it can be later used. Pour the blended pepper and the sliced onions into the yam and shake the pot so the pepper can be well mixed with the yams. Cover the pot and reduce the heat to cook for 5 minutes.

7. After 5 minutes, add the oil then stir with wooden spoon to mix the peppers and slightly mash it.

8. Add the corned beef and continue mashing it. The mashing can slightly be done or intensely based on once preference.

9. Taste to be sure the seasoning is ok, if not it can be adjusted.

10. Cover and let it cook on a low heat for another 5-10 minutes. It should be ready now.

11. Porridge is now ready and it can be served with plantains, chicken, beef or fried fish☺.

# Fish Soup

This is one delicious meal that can either be eaten alone as appetizer or be eaten along with other food like rice, plantain, eba, etc. To cook fish soup you can use Fresh Tilapia, Catfish, Mackerel, or any fish of your choice.

## Ingredients

- 3 medium size Tilapia fish (Clean and cut into 3 pieces each)
- 3 Red bell peppers
- 5 medium size Tomatoes or 2 8oz cans of Tomato sauce
- 1-3 Habanero peppers
- 1 medium size bulb onions
- 1 -1 ½ cup of vegetable or canola oil
- 1 teaspoon of salt
- 6 cubes of knorr (it's a well-known Nigeria seasoning – but you can use any of your choice)
- 1 tablespoon of curry

## How to cook

1. Put the fish in a clean bowl and season with 1 teaspoon of salt, ½ tablespoon of curry, 3 cubes of knorr. Put the well-seasoned fish in the fridge so it can marinate while you preparing the soup.

2. Blend all the peppers (Red bell peppers, fresh tomatoes or tomatoes sauce, habanero peppers and the onions) till it is well smooth like a paste.

3. Once done, set your stove to medium heat and place a clean pot on it, add the oil and let it heat for a minute. Then pour the well-blended peppers.

4. Add the remaining ½ teaspoon of curry (this is optional), add the knorr cubes, stir and cover. Let it cook for 15-20 minutes on a medium heat

5. After 20 minutes, open the lid, stir and then taste – to see if it no longer taste fresh but cooked. More seasonings can be added if need be.

6. The next is to gently put the fish one after the other to avoid it squishing. Once all the fish has been put in the soup, shake the pot so the soup can cover the fish.

7. If the soup looks too thick, you can add little water (I like my fish soup a bit thick, not watery and not too thick☺).

8. Cover and let it cook for 10-20 minutes

9. Now it is ready☺. Enjoy alone or with other meals.

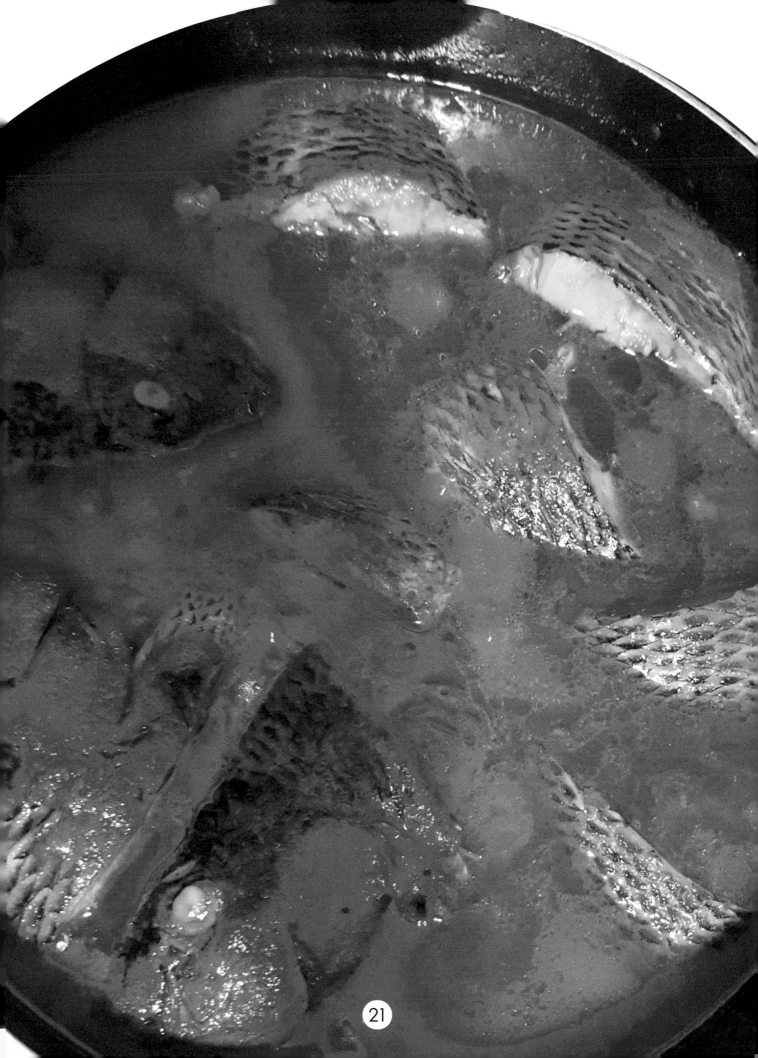

# Tips on using Microwave for quick cooking

This is just quick tips of using the microwave to make fast meal known as lazy cooking. It is important that you use plastics or bowl that are microwaveable and also lid or cover as required.

## Microwave Moimoi (Beans pudding)

To do that, mix all your ingredients together (beans paste, seasonings, corn beef, fresh egg and vegetable or canola oil). Once all well-mixed, pour into a microwaveable plastic (Use a plastic that has lid). Add the boiled sliced eggs. Cover with the lid and place in the microwave for 2 minutes at first. Check to see if it is cooked, if not place it back and let it cook for another 1 minute. It is important that you slow cook it after the first 2 minutes by adding 1 minute intermittently if needed so as to avoid it been over cooked. Once it is well cooked, then it is ready to eat ☺

## Microwave Eba

Get a clean bowl, add water and garri – let the water be above the garri. Place in the microwave, cover and let it cook for 2 minutes at first. Bring out, mix the garri together. Place it back in the microwave for another 1 minutes. Bring out and stir it still it is well mixed. If not that cooked, place it back for another 30 seconds to 1 minute.

## Using Microwave to harden boiled Egg

This can be done when the boiled egg is not well cooked. Instead of throwing it away or eating not well cooked egg, put the egg in a microwaveable bowl and add water. Place it in the oven for 30 secs, if still not cooked to your satisfaction; place it back for another 30 secs. Now it should be well cooked to eat.

# Using Microwave to pre-cook pepper

I usually do this when I am running late with my cooking and I need to use pepper to make sardine or corned beef stew. I blend my peppers not too smooth. Then I pour it in a plastic and place it in the microwave for 3-5 minutes. This will pre-cook it and hasten the frying for making stew.

# Microwave to make Semo

Pour the semo in a microwaveable bowl; add butter, a pinch of salt and water. Mix together to a slightly watery consistency. Place in the microwave for 3 minutes. Bring it out and stir till it is smooth. If it does not taste well cooked, put it in the microwave again for 2 minutes till it taste and looked cooked.

Printed in the United States
By Bookmasters